Woman on the Edge

Imogen Lace

© 2010 Imogen Lace. All rights reserved.

ISBN 978-1-4717-8165-0

© Cover Artwork by Tracy Swift

Imogen Publications

First Published in 2010

Produced by Lulu

Introduction

I was born in Hamilton Lodge, Hyde Park Doncaster on 9th June 1964. For the next 11 years I travelled with my family on the fairgrounds. We travelled around Yorkshire and the North East. We spent the winter months in Chapeltown near Sheffield, which is where me and my sister, Anne, went to school. I loved going to school and joined the Brownies. We had a coach-built living wagon with polished sides and brass knobs. Brown Owl once came to our living van to see the brass knobs and witness me cleaning them for which I was given a badge to sew onto my uniform. I was proud.

When I was 11 me and my family moved and settled down in Cudworth, Barnsley, South Yorkshire. My Dad bought an Amusement Arcade and Café which we all worked in and lived in the flat above. I went to school at Snydale Road and then Willowgarth High School until I was 15. By that time Imelda, my younger sister was still in education at Ackworth boarding School and my sister, Anne, was standing the Markets at Barnsley with Chamois leathers and household goods. At Christmas she sold wrapping paper, tinsel, cards, and gifts.

I worked for my dad until I was about 19, then I got a flat in Barnsley and got a job with Ross's Ice cream – which was short-lived. I then got involved with the Barnsley Community Productions Theatre Group. I co-wrote a play called, "Soap Opera", and then I went back to college to do 3 'A' Levels in Psychology, Communications, and English Literature. I went on from there to study Drama and Theatre Studies at University of Kent at Canterbury. I met friends there who I still keep in touch with. I lived in Whitstable and finished a year's study. Then I went with some friends to London. We wanted to live in London for our year 'out' of study.

London was brilliant. I met John who became my boyfriend for the next 2 years. He had organised a book and record distribution based in Hackney Downs. He knew a lot of people and got me a job in a whole food shop on Saturdays and I got a job in the week cycle couriering in the same company John was working for. We had to learn the 'knowledge' and I maintained my bicycle very well for the job. I lived in a house with five other women who all rode bikes, had jobs, and went to college.

I decided to try my hand at carpentry and took on a training course at Lambeth Women's Workshop near Brixton. It was a City & Guilds which lasted 6 months but, I only did 3 and went into working with children with special needs – which was a most rewarding job.

I spent 3 years in London, which was full and fast. I was still visiting Whitstable at weekends and eventually my friends agreed that I should move back. So I did and got a job waitressing in Beanies Mexican Restaurant. I got a flat and enjoyed the next few years living in Whitstable, painting and singing with my guitar. I knew the musicians and artists crowd and felt part of that community, living on my own as many of my women friends did.

For a while I worked at the Umbrella Centre in Whitstable, which was a Community Centre. We put on a play of Brecht's and I worked in the Art Room. We were trying to set up an Arts & Drama Centre but, we didn't succeed and someone from the Social Services came to replace us in our endeavours and they set up an Arts & Drama Centre from the work we had done – which was positive.

In 2004 I decided to go back to University and put all my papers in for Archaeology and Law. I had moved out of Island Wall, where I had a bedsit and was staying with friends, looking for a flat in Herne Bay near my cousin's Amusement Arcade. I finally found one on Sea Street but, it was going to be a month before I could move in. So I was staying with a friend, Valerie Carless, in her flat in Tankerton which had a spare bedroom, but after a couple of weeks Valerie got a proper lodger and I was moved to the sofa. However, there wasn't much room for the four of us. That bout of homelessness was a hard one. I should have gone up to Barnsley and stayed with my family before moving into the flat, but I really didn't want to bother them and I thought I could look for a job and get some study in before term started. Staying at Valerie's was a good laugh and her boyfriend always had jokes and general mirth. She is a good woman with a lot of good women friends, like me.

At that time I bumped into Mick Field, who I knew from the Road Protest which had happened a few years earlier. They were all good and sound people on the Road Protest, though it was never won and the road went through. Mick said there were rooms going at a squat hotel for £30 per week. He gave me his number and I said I'd have a think about it. I think it was better for our friendship that I gave her her living room space back – being as she had a lodger now. I ended up moving into the hotel with two weeks to go before I moved into the flat on sea street. If I had known then, what I know now, I would never have taken a room there.

There was no hot water, the rubbish was building up outside, and the cellar was flooding… and no lock on my room door. I had lived in squats for three years in London where we did maintenance and organised a food co-op to be delivered once a month. We all had work to do on the places and designated a day a week to work on the house. In this hotel, there was nothing like that going on. I don't know where their heads were at but the accumulation of the rubbish outside caused it to get an article in the local newspaper as an eyesore and no one defended the place with the newspaper. So, after a week or so of nobody saying anything, I was ready to go. And then, the caretaker said to me, "If you haven't got the rent next week I've got a client for you who could do with some 'servicing'." I laughed nervously and went up to my room, packing my stuff and trying to phone friends to help. What a situation I'd got myself in! It was time to get out!

By the time I moved into my new flat on Sea Street, I was hearing voices and was getting confused. I became so ill that I was having stomach problems and had to go to the doctor's for some medicine. My plans for going to University were getting further away as my confusion about the voices and what I now call 'psychic attacks' were getting worse. It seemed like every night cars would pass by the flat and people would shout, "Slut", "Jew" and "Gippo". It was that real, that I went to the Police, who just gave me a victim support card for an office in Canterbury that was only open a few hours. The Police couldn't help and it continued. I was being harassed. This was the start of it.

Imogen

Woman On The Edge

I hear voices but do not agree with the medication, or at the way people get treated under the mental health service. I am not mad, I don't even believe in the schizophrenia labels but this whole episode of hearing voices has driven me to write something.

I try to seek help where I can but the nature of the voices, persecutory, are making me fear for my life as in the last 5 years since the onslaught, the rape, they have continued to borage me with abuse. I have been to 3 or 4 voices hearing meetings now and found some strength in Dr Dirk Corstens's construct he performed on me. Here it is:

Imogen   London 21-4-2009

Imogen is 44-years old. She lives independently, has a boyfriend and is in psychiatric treatment since 2004. After a date rape she started to hear voices. Nobody believed her story and she was sent to a psychiatric hospital, where she stayed for 6 months. She has to take a depot every 2 weeks (community treatment order?).

The identity of the voices

Imogen hears numerous voices that she differentiates:
1. Zac, male 28 years old
2. Shea, female 28 years old
3. A group of voices, identified as friends of Zac
4. A crowd identified as fascists
5. Her family
6. Linette

The characteristics of the voices

1. The voice of the rapist, every 3 months. He is Catholic (Imogen C of E). He expresses hatred.
2. A woman, friend of Zac. Powerful with Zac.
3. They say they rule the pubs in a special area
4. Fascists who want to eradicate gipsies and people from the fairgrounds; called 'the mob' by Shea, every day
5. Father and mother incidentally, especially her sister, once a month. Her sister gives advices.
6. Only once, a former unfriendly CPN

The content of the voices

1. I am going to murder you – You will die for the country – Get a link
2. You look good tonight. They are the mob.
3. Same as 4.
4. We're gonna murder you and your family – we start a pub war
5. Sister: Take a bath. Don't stay too long. Come straight back.
6. Screamed against Imogen

Triggers

When I try to write, when I want to express myself.

The history of the voices

Back in 2004 Imogen was with friends one evening. She already knew Zac vaguely. Her invited her to stay overnight because it was too late to go back home. Imogen had no intention for whatever intimacy. When she awoke in the morning she felt awful and discovered that she was drugged and raped, presumably by Zac. She became very scared. She heard a crowd in the house walking downstairs and was terrified. She ran away and only some days later she could find the balance to go to the police. Instead of investigating the sexual abuse they sent her to a psychiatric hospital when she complained about the 'psychic attacks' Zac still performed.

At that time Imogen had a lot of friends, was happy, worked part-time, she had no partner and planned to go back to University in order to take up another study. The rape was an emotional overwhelming event that Imogen couldn't handle. Nothing else happened that otherwise could explain the emotional turmoil Imogen got in the period thereafter.

Childhood history

Imogen originates from the fairground community. Her family travelled through the country. When she was eleven her father started an Amusement Arcade and they started to live in a regular house. Imogen worked for her father from very young on. The fairground community is a close community that has certain rules and many secrets. When Imogen was 17 years old she had an abortion. The father of her unborn child was a 22-year old boy from the community. Imogen felt she was too young to have a child. The only one who knew about the abortion was her best girlfriend. She didn't tell her parents at that time. She left the fairground community from that time. Both emotionally and practically I assume. In 1987 (22 years old) she went to University to study theatre. She had several relationships. Her passion was to write songs. Guilt about the abortion and leaving her community appear to play an important role now. At that time it seemed insignificant. To me Imogen appeared to be an extravert and spontaneous person who enjoyed live and never thought much about herself. The rape must have destroyed her personality temporarily, although the way she talked this day you could clearly see the woman she must have been before. Someone who takes life for what it is, and was capable of quickly overcoming disappointments and take new directions. The abuse though was too overwhelming and she was not able to handle emotionally. Difficult emotions are now represented by the voices.

Who represent the voices
1. Zac, the rapist.
2. Shea, a friend of Zac.

3. The friends of Zac (probably the people that Imogen heard coming down the stairs when she was so terrified?)
4. These three represent the rape, the violation of her personal integrity, the damage done to her body. Although Imogen probably didn't experience the rape consciously, her body remembers. Nobody listened to her traumatic story, she was declared mad, unrighteously. The police never investigated what really happened and rejected thereby her personal integrity. Another severe trauma.
5. People who hate foreigners and gipsies, people from the fairground and Jews (amongst others). This represents her origins, the (covered) hatred of society towards people from the fairgrounds. Imogen never was very conscious of this, because she knows it is unjustified. But unconsciously she probably must have felt it. The rape re-actualised this discriminatory stand of the general public. Probably this also represents Imogen's feelings of unsafety towards her community, that didn't support her properly when she was pregnant by the boy from that community. At a very young age Imogen had to make a very difficult decision, and must have felt very alone in that decision. Guilt feelings after an abortion are very usual. Her community and she herself didn't acknowledge that. It determined her future in both positive and negative ways.
6. Her family. These voices support her. They may represent her dependency on her family, that she loves but is also ambivalent to. They supported her in the past but at a very significant moment Imogen seemed not capable and they were not capable of supporting her in her very difficult decision.
7. Linette. She represents Imogen's feelings towards the specific CPN who she felt threatened by and more generally towards psychiatry who rejects her story, her as a person and forces her to take medication without addressing the traumas Imogen experienced.

What problems do the voices represent

We didn't explore this together enough, so I try to make an inventory of my thoughts. If you don't agree just throw it away. Maybe some thoughts do appeal to you.

Imogen discovered that the voices represent several unresolved conflicts:
- The unresolved trauma of the rape (being damaged, no justice done).
- The unresolved feelings around the abortion (grief and guilt.
- The unresolved rejection by her original community (left alone.
- Unresolved fear for the general public who tend to discriminate minorities, to which Imogen apparently belongs (covert hatred). Unresolved justification of what had happened to her, the police did reject her like the fascists tend to do.
- Imogen's positive approach to life and people in general, maybe a naïve stance, too trustfully believe in other people. Not being able to express feelings of rejection and anger in an adequate way. Difficulties in finding the right people who can really give her support.

Some considerations towards a treatment plan

Generally we consider three steps in the treatment of people hearing voices.
1. The most hindering aspects of the voices. We didn't explore this enough, but it certainly needs attention. I couldn't find out what hinders you the most.
2. Emotional problems that underly the voices and excercise with it. I guess that finding trust in other people again is an important task. Learning to express anger on the one hand and your vulnerablity

(dependence of others, feelings of rejection and needs) on the other side.
3. Working through trauma and feelings of shame and guilt. This I think is the most important thing. Find someone who really takes you seriously and listens to you and helps you to express your feelings of guilt, loss and shame. Learning to talk about your emotions, like you did this day in front of an audience.

Dear Imogen, I hope this will help you. I found you very brave! You deserve a better treatment and should go for it!

If you want to correspond about this, feel free. I will try to reply as best I can.

Dirk Corstens

Karen Taylor:

I have read the documents & made a few spelling & grammar changes. I am not sure about the bit about her community not supporting her when she had the abortion, as she kept it secret so they couldn't support her, now they know they haven't rejected her for it. I think its her own guilt she finds difficult she didn't have the baby as she wanted a different life, she left the community to become different , thereby rejecting her family internally , now the outside world has proven dangerous she is left with the "what if" feeling that if she hadn't gone off she would now have her own family , would not be mad etc. etc. , through personal similar experience I wonder also if she ever grieved for the baby properly , but repressed these feelings, , now reawakened as voices call her a killer also the sense of guilt and shame could be saying to her that the rape was punishment for killing her own child.

The voice of the sister could also represent Imogen's own "sensible self" as externalised self-talk, be careful, go home...

I am really sorry I couldn't stay longer the session was so gripping. Everyone who has contacted me for the PowerPoint has said how much they enjoyed the day.

I really enjoyed my 2 days with you.

Dirk:

Thanks for the changes you made, but especially your comments that make much sense. It would have been great as we could have such a discussion with Imogen herself! Next time we should do this together, it can be very fruitful.

To the content of your comments, I want to reply that your view would be very valuable in a discussion to promote Imogen's own thinking. Two views that are options; not contradictory.

You're right SHE kept it secret at the end, but the reason for this secretiveness could be, in my opinion, that she didn't feel much supported by her family. She expected rejection. Indeed, guilt and grief play a role; the 'what if' reasoning she also expressed ("I would be a mom with twelve kids"). She indeed didn't grieve for her unborn child, the 'killing' of her child. And in symbolic voices-language this could easily become punishment for killing her own child; Very clever. I would hold on the view that the voice of her sister represents her need for support from her family but, at the same time, you are right in that at the end voices are representations of own internal motives, capacities, and needs.

Eventually, and I don't know if you were still there at that moment, Imogen and I concluded that there were many unresolved things; too much to address all. I had the impression she envisaged that there will be a lot of work to do.

~

They got it wrong about my family not supporting me through the abortion, I simply didn't tell them so they weren't able to help. I didn't really leave the fairground. I always have my cousins who I still help on the fairgrounds – traditionally at Halifax Gala which has always been held on the week of my birthday, June 9th.

Whatever I write down, the voices always say, "you haven't said enough". So anyways, I'll just go with the flow of how I can address these problems or unresolved feelings but, I will not keep feeling guilt about what my voices say. I made a positive decision to have an abortion and it is every woman's right in this society to seek abortion if the child is not wanted. There are many reasons why women don't want to have children at an early age and I was 17.

I didn't ask to be raped, and I was completely innocent in believing that where I was I was safe, and I blindly trusted the rapist. Anyhow, I wrote a story about it all in the early days and finished it recently. Here it is...

Woman on the Edge

The voice hearers groups she had been attending had all said it was the trauma of the rape that brought it all on, all the different voices, but she couldn't believe that totally, she still felt that they were psychic attacks with threats on her life daily made her all too anxious about the state as well as her fears for her life, the voices were always telling her they were in control and asking her to do things then saying there was a month left to live. She was told this all the time, "we're gonna do a murder and it's you", they told her nearly everyday.

James thinks all the abuse and name calling is character assassination, saying there's a month left of the abuse so it was like a sentence.

Jakie Dillon from the voice hearers said you had to take note and listen to the voices and more or less that it was no use in 'dampening them down' with medication. Now she was trying to write something down and they were saying what do you think happens once you've droned on about it, as if what she thought about herself made no difference to the voices, they were still saying she had a month left and that they had licked her soul, this made her want to write down something about her childhood, how good it was.

It was a fact that the Voices Hearing Network said that the voices can come from many sources – birds or other animals, the rustling of leaves, traffic noise, banging hot water pipes, crowd noise, machinery noise, and even air conditioning. The most common explanations from voice hearers are that they are voices of spirits, of dead people, daemons, angels, telepathy, God-like beings, unidentified invisible beings, from other dimensions or planets and the professional explanations of voices are: Voices come from the brain, or that voices are from the tricks of the mind when it is bored or under influence of suggestion.

Her own explanation was that it was telepathy. The voices were persecutory in the eyes of the professionals. But to her, they were giving the illusion that she was under Political pressure in that, they were saying words of abuse and threatening her life every day. She was aware that she lived in another world from her voices and that these threats of crowds being against her were not really real and in her confusion, she tried to write to express these feelings of persecution. So that maybe, there would be some comfort in other people knowing that these were small-minded fascistic type people and violent in their threats. She had not enough evidence to file a rape charge against the rapist. All she had was her own words in the confusion of theirs.

~

"Paranoid pikey slut" said the rapist. She thought about it, paranoid pikey slut, she had feelings of paranoia because of the murder threats, but as for the "pikey slut", she knew she was fighting a verbal attack that was derogatory yet, 'pikey' was not recognised as racist, it was said like 'gypsy', and she had been called a gypsy before, when she was very young at infant and junior school in High Green – but not for years. She thought of how lucky she had been living with people who were 'politically correct' at a time when she was politicising herself. She knew she was a green ecologist, a Community Arts worker and supporter; she remembered one of the German women saying there was no such thing as Community Arts in Germany because they didn't need it. How peculiar, she thought.

She thought of how the rape had instilled her with the violence they committed against her and she knew they were out to prey on her for the effect of the novelty of her being from the fairgrounds; being a feminist and being a 'sinner'. At any rate, she was beginning to look outside of the religious guilt trip and outside of the patriarchy of her upbringing – simply because they were standing against her rights. The abortion stuff was heavy enough to have to keep considering the arguments, for and against. It was political and she had respected her father's ways. Although she hadn't yet married herself and both her sisters were married, she hadn't seen it as being oppressive until now. She knew she needed some legal guidance and like-minded support to defend herself now she had been targeted; maybe a feminist lawyer. After all, millions of other women go through that situation in their lives when they have to make the choice. They shouldn't have to be guilt tripped about it!

The violent stuff had made her uneasy about her writing. She had always used it cathartically but, the paranormal made her think it was all just some 'paranoid' fun on a hard-core level and she just wasn't getting the joke of it; as if she had made all the voices up; recognisable people like the rapist; and the others. But she knew that wasn't how it really was. Descriptions of violent acts against her and the psychological abuse were paralysing her senses. She could feel herself being physically threatened and it terrified her and it terrified her to think about writing it down. Could she use her creativity as she had done in the past, before the rape? She was annoyed again about the violation and annoyed at herself again for being so naive and trusting in the first place; for ever having been in that stupid situation. She remembered the time she became aware that her sense of humour was different to theirs. The caretaker had said, "If you haven't got the rent I've a client here..." She had laughed it off with him and realised that it may have been a joke to her but the guy was serious – and he was saying it to help her if she had no money – but she had pushed it to the back of her mind, thinking that she would be moving out in a few days, so she wouldn't have to think about that kind of thing in her life. It had scared her. Afterwards, they said she had been living in a dream world.

This time she didn't go away with the fairies. This time she was seeing through the whole conspiracy like it was a mirror into another world. Could this be crazy? The arguments about 'primitive' and 'civilised' ways of thinking the 'in between'. She remembered 'A Clockwork Orange' by Anthony Burgess and the culture that Alex had built around his violent attacks; the linguistics of the book; the made up terminology that was cultivated around his gang; the banning of the film because of the rape scene; the association that 'Singing In The Rain' had with that scene, whenever she had heard it on TV or on the radio. She had to face the fact that she had been a victim of the 'primitive' stuff. 'Civilised' didn't really come into it. She thought they were psychotic generally and were using drugs to enhance what they were doing to her. It was all for their fun, like 'The Droogs' in Burgess's story. She had seen the play 'Clockwork Orange 2000' at Drury Lane with Phil Daniels as Alex and a very grandiose set with a giant bust of Beethoven, and a scene with riot police that was well choreographed, and afterwards she and Jon had got the soundtrack to the movie. She had had a fleeting ambition to write something in a similar way about a group of women who were out for peace instead of violence, with a 'Soya Miloko Bar' and terminology based around the whole food stuff and non-violent direct action. She remembered her 3 years with Jon, the learning together, the healthy lifestyle they had, the cycling everywhere around London, and all the films, plays and music they had been into – like 'Betty Blue'. The soundtrack to that film is so heart-wrenching when you listen to it and think of Betty and her sad situation, but it had been a favourite film of theirs.

"The public are coming to whack the slut", said the rapist. She had had hours of different voices saying what they thought of her. This was all because of the lies they had built up around the truth of her personal history. She thought of how they had got together and set her up with all this stuff; how they said they wanted her death or her in prison or sat up at the hospital where they could continue psychically attacking her. They went on and on about it; how they had made her into 'the slut' to be scorned. She thought of a programme she had watched where Toyah Wilcox goes into a past life and finds she was a woman who had been made to sit in a room underneath a church and people from the town come and say things to her as some kind of punishment in mediaeval times. Maybe this was a modern day equivalent. Whatever the reasons she had to take account she was a person, a citizen with rights, not to be abused in this way. She just couldn't fathom out why the crimes committed against her were being glorified and no-one gave a damn about rape, the post traumatic stress, or the subsequent terrorisation she was experiencing from this defamation of character. The police were saying there wasn't enough evidence to charge the rapist – let alone caution him for the murder threats and damage that he had done to her and her family in their home town with their lies, racist views, hypocrisy, prejudices and the violence they were threatening.

They were going on about terrorism again – the lie they had brandished her with. She could see that society was so paranoid about national security that they wanted to place the blame on someone. She could see that this lie was 'topical' and absolutely ludicrous in reality. She was as concerned about terrorism against the country by fundamentalists as anyone was but, not paranoid as she was hearing people were about Muslims in general. She thought that the whole culture was being blamed in our society – breeding suspicion and mistrust in communities instead of unity and tolerance between the creeds against terrorism. Yet it seemed, with all the Internet access to the wars, the availability of this stuff to anyone – children included – that society was becoming more violent itself and to talk about peace was just not 'PC' anymore. She remembered a peace demonstration she went to in Canterbury, where men were shouting stuff as they drove by in their cars. "Nuke the bastards!" shouted one guy... and general stuff about using violence rather than peace. It was discouraging but, that is the way people are reacting since the war has become part of the national psyche. But it has to be recognised that most religious faiths do not agree with killing people and that these fundamentalists have got to have been brainwashed to believe all that stuff.

She thought about the Conscientious Objectors in the World Wars; how Wilfred Owen and Siegfried Sassoon had written about the war whilst they were in the trenches, and after with poems about the 'futility' of war, which she had read during her 'A' levels, the peace movement had caught her conscience and sensibility before she had visited Greenham with a group of students from Uni. She had continued to attend peace demos and regarded the CND with some respect. A poster and T-shirt design that Jon had, said, "war is not healthy for children or other living things". Simple and true – though this interest in the saving of human lives needs numbers and for the thousands of people that turned out against the war, there were thousands that didn't. Many people believe that the act of going to war has caused more terrorist threats against our country. Whatever, we are all most certainly living with 'paranoid' ideas about the security of our towns and cities and about who in our communities are the real terrorists. After all, 'scaremongering' was a terrorist act that she herself was a victim of. She had made up a new word for it. A part of the psychological terrorism she was experiencing through the paranormal could be seen as 'Para-psychological warfare', as they had said it was a war on her because of her background; the 'pikey' thing that they had used to torment her in a nature of 'persecution'.

Now, even the public were telling her she was a victim of 'fate'. What a load of complete and utter bullshit she thought. She could feel them all with their small minds pinning her down to their own self-gratifications; using her to satisfy their own suspicions and doubts; a single woman, been in hospital, lived in London. Whatever paranoid reasons the rapist and his gang had given to them, she knew that she had been made a scapegoat. She knew that they took all sorts of drugs to wind themselves up to the states of violent threats and attacks and that they were making stuff up because they were prejudiced and found her to be the 'novelty' they needed to use as their vehicle to gain some notoriety. And she knew it was a war because they kept calling her a 'Jew' and preying on her with verbal abuse and violent threats. She wasn't a Jew and she thought they were calling her that to give themselves more reasons to inflict their hatred on her as being from another culture. It was actually the Showmen they were trying to attack, through her, and she felt again that it was a mixture of jealousy, ignorance, fear and their lust for power; that they had discredited her and were using her for their own ends. She hadn't lived her life up to now, learned about religious fanaticism, systems of ritual and belief from an anthropological perspective, and women's rights, to have some paranoid rapist using this stuff to do her harm. He had already done enough to make her a physical wreck.

"That's enough", said the rapist, as she started to write. "You're a paranoid Jew". She thought of Sylvia Plaith and how depressing her poetry was. Largely she thought because she came just before the on serge of the new feminist writers, where the structure of subject matter was based around the fight against the subordination of women in our society – a more positive perspective on the women's role than the negativity of being persecuted in a situation of war. She had found her own attempt at poetry of late was just as depressing as Plaith's – in the mode of being victimised and not the kind of literature that she had wanted to pen but, this stuff was coming at her from morning until she eventually got to sleep and it was difficult for her to rise above the experience – having so many people on her case all the time over the last 7 months. She really did feel oppressed by it all and in this modern society, with all the hindsight we had from the Hitler experience, the equal rights for women, the rape crisis centres, the women's refuges, all the demonstrating she had done for various causes – she now needed help from somewhere. She thought about the Prime Minister, the Queen... the Police, again. She wasn't really sure where to take this. It was a violation of human rights and she had suffered enough for the sin of abortion – never mind being slandered with the other stuff. The public humiliation of it all was enough.

They were calling her a "whacked ho". She certainly understood that she had been being whacked down for the last 2 years because she was spirited and could see through all their pretentions. But as for the "ho" bit, she wasn't sure what it meant to the rapist. She supposed he had thought of her as a prostitute and had his mates pay to rape her after she had been drugged. "You're a porn star" they had said 2 years ago. They said that they had taken pictures and shown them to the army in Canterbury but, she hadn't really believed it. Maybe it was true and this is why things had got so bad for her now. She had never had sex for money. Her boyfriends, mostly long term, were people she had loved and shared a relationship with. After all this stuff, it seemed that they were saying she was a 'reprobate' because she wouldn't go out and be a prostitute for them. It wasn't in her conscience and perhaps that is why they were saying she "hadn't got enough love". She had thought her love was given in her creative life as well as everyday relationships with friends and family, though she knew she was at a loss at their saying it was a "hate campaign". She had always been a friendly and confident person before all this; had been brought up working with the public and was good with children; always thinking that one day she would have her own family. Anyhow, she knew where her energy was being channelled when she was playing music, writing or painting. She saw it as being in control of her own life, or at least having a creative life parallel to the everyday stuff.

She laughed to herself at the thought of how much money she could have earned if all this stuff was true. The commodity stuff, the exploitation stuff but, accepting all this, she felt her soul was being suffocated. Seeing through the stuff made her feel less of a 'reprobate'. The rapist had held the power in the transference of violence (in the rape) and the projection of his theory that she was all these terrible things (through verbal abuse). Her only self-defence against this violation was the ability to listen. What they had concocted was a threat to her career prospects in the professional world; that is why they were constantly putting her down with their bigotry, hypocrisies and fabrications. She had to admit it was a really good stitch up on someone. She could see the power of lies unfolding; a kind of "get out of that one". What an evil-minded way to get oneself into the North she thought – "my home town". And she did feel conscious about the psychic attacks and the things they had said they had told the town about her; the lies; the defamation of character; the very personal stuff in her history. She knew she had to get a good lawyer to defend her against this slander and to stop the rapist and his gang in their evil endeavours.

She did see it was a 'war' on her because of her background and that's why they made threats of violence and murder towards her. She thought they were psychotic despots using drugs and fear to exert power over her; she could hear it in the rapist's voice; the changing of his mood swings in the verbal attacks; it terrified her. After one very severe attack that had lasted all day, she called the police again to make another statement but there wasn't enough evidence. It was like a conspiracy against her; like they were letting them get away with it. She wanted him convicted for this crime; she wanted everyone to know what a rapist he was and what he and his gang were up to. She was prepared to stand up for the fairground and for her rights; prepared to defend herself because she knew she had had good friends who had known her over the years. She knew she had goals and prospects before the rape and she knew she had plenty more to give – and if that all had to be put into the fight then so be it.

~

Now she was back in the hospital and all those paranoia's about the rapist saying that she was an enemy of the people became just a sick joke. She knew the nurses there were in the caring profession and should be used to the policies of not passing judgement but more or less looking after the patients. She was safe from the threats of physical violence but, there was too much time to postulate on their saying: "You getting linked off" (Suicide). Why did everyone sound so paranoid? It was depressing for her that these people were hell bent on causing her mental harm by taunting and venting their angers and own political frustrations on her, as if she hadn't thought about stuff, as if she couldn't see why they used people in their own evil games of victimisation. It was a political truth that everyone gets frustrated about stuff in their lives. After all, there is only so much you can take before you have to stand up and say something, try do something about it to make a change. She really felt like she should have done something in that way. She thought of the times she wanted to be in a band – to stand up and say something – but she was older now. There were other ways to say something.

"End it all with a ring pull." They were saying. It was all like a paranoid dream. People, including children, shouting at her as if they had walked this earth long enough to verbally abuse an adult. She felt demoralised again. Other people on the ward were having their own troubles and she tried to focus on what was important in her life, now that things were more routine in her daily life. She had planned on visiting the gym but, was out of sync with the timetable. She had planned occupational therapy to channel her creativity into design and art therapy and looked forward to making large scale models of beautiful things. Her creative life had come back through the wilderness; the 'teenage wasteland' of her formative youth had made her understand that creativity was important for the mind, body and soul – just like music, whether listening to it or playing it, and there were spaces in the day to focus a little at a time, yet the pressure wasn't gone.

She wasn't sorry for demonstrating against the eviction of a whole estate in East London; she wasn't sorry for wanting peace; for going to Greenham; for loving; for sharing ideas; for communal living; for working for a co-operative; for being spiritually married to her ideal partners; for having spiritual accountability toward some kind of fellow-ship between peoples of the world and the creeds. "Think globally – act locally", she remembered was a slogan on a t-shirt she had worn in her London days, and she wondered again, "how could she make peace, after such violations of her rights, as a woman, as a citizen, as a person, because of the rape?" There was such global injustice in the world, such violent attitudes toward minorities and subcultures in our society. Where do you start?

It was her ward round meeting. Everything had been going well since she had been admitted. She had got on with some of the things she had wanted to – given the situation she was in, having to stay in hospital. She had felt confident that her named nurse had said that she would 'put it to her Doctor that things were going well' and ask if she 'could stay there as a voluntary patient'. She was feeling good about that. However, as soon as she stepped in the room she was met by about 8 different people. Her named nurse wasn't there! The Doctor seemed like he had something he wanted to say before sorting out the overnight leaves and hours off the ward, so she sat and listened. He said she had an illness and that it was schizophrenia. She could feel herself sinking down into the chair under the intense observation of them all. It was demoralising, after such a good week. The Doctor hadn't even been anywhere near her since the last meeting; "he didn't even know her", she thought.

She thought about 'fight or flight'. She had been fighting in every given situation of late, and the 'pecking order' of animalism; the fact that she had been a victim and the fact that some people were treating her as such... although the incident was over in a sense. She just felt left with the scars. This all could have rendered her debilitated like the psychic attacks had, but she had a friend, James, who had been there to help her through it over the last few months. He was there when the Doctors and Police had come around to her house. It was very oppressive meeting all those people again who didn't really understand what was happening to her. No real help, no arrest of the rapist, no cautioning the gang for their constant harassment. She had an inkling that they may have spoken to the rapist and that he had given them the same charismatic bunch of bullshit lies that he had been telephoning her with for the past 8 months now.

There was another woman on the ward who was getting violent threats and hassle from a group of attackers on the paranormal level. She was younger than Imogen and had been raped – though she didn't know if it was the same people who were harassing her now. They told her to do violent acts and to kill herself. After one particularly bad night Imogen had tried to comfort her saying that they weren't actually there, something she had had said to her when she was being psychically attacked, but she didn't say, "it's all in your head", as she had had said to her. At any rate she was aware that she was in some sort of personal war with these people and that she wasn't the only one, although each persons paranormal lives was personal to them. She guessed that was why it was difficult for the mainstream psychiatrists to deal with. They can't really do anything about it; they call it, 'episodic psychosis' and 'schizophrenia'.

Being put into a category like this made her think of the dualities of her life; the joys and the pains; the studious times and the creative times; the music and art in her life. She had to try and channel her feelings creatively in music as well as art.

~

She was in hospital under section 3 of the Mental Health Act. She thought how ridiculous it was how they had taken her into the hospital – 3 doctors and 2 police officers. She was sure she had heard one of them say something to make her more aware of what the 'crew' say they were doing to her on the paranormal, was actually going on in her life. What a mess, the way it had all gone over the last 3 or so years with her life; in and out of the paranormal and the hospital. How could she protect herself from what Zac and his 'crew', as they kept calling themselves, had done since the rape? She was still suffering the psychic attacks under their lies and views on her own choices in life. The past was in the past as far as the abortions were concerned. She had mourned and cried and felt guilty for too long over all that since they had guilt tripped her. She knew she had not been ready to have a child and had reasons at that time, when she was young and life was different. She had career plans, supportive friends, and she had not told her family. She should not have to be guilt tripped for something that was her right to choose; something that millions of other women go through. Theirs was a narrow view and they lied about things that would discredit her character. She was fully aware of that by now.

She had decided against telling the doctors what was happening to her on the paranormal because it had got her absolutely nowhere as far as the attacks were concerned, and the internet had led her to thinking about contacting a shaman or a priest to try to protect and defend herself against them. None of the voices were very nice except for Steve's – who only said anything ever, twice or so. He had asked her: "Now why'd ya go and get yerself murdered?" in his light-hearted southern accent. She had almost laughed when he had spoken, but it was really too grim. The living hope she had in her consciousness of her experience in Kent; and she knew she had gone back home to Yorkshire to stay with the love he had given to her over the years, close at heart. Now that illusion was shattering under the pressure of the attacks, the slander, the threats, the aggressiveness, in people around her. Was this really happening? Yes, it was real. What a nightmare. She remembered when she first heard them on a bus going to London from Barnsley. They were playing her a tune and she had thought it was someone's headphones... then it happened again. It was 'episodic', as the labels in psychiatry say.

The truth seemed to be, that her creative life was being thwarted by the force of the attacks all around her. They were aggressive and threatening and she had felt the 'fight or flight' situation, but was unable to fly because of the shackles that were surrounding her in the system, She wanted to run her own business, to prove to herself that she could make a success out of all she had learned about food, catering and health stuff. This was where her own feelings of self-worth were... at some 'schizophrenic' clash! She felt herself that her strength had been as an artist and had always been buzzing with ideas for new paintings, incorporating different religious and artistic symbols, maybe futuristic and surreal... as were some of her short story ideas. She had read some science-fiction written by women and held the belief of the utopian ethics of the mind, to be able to look at society from without as well as within, as if you were an anthropologist looking at society as a structure of symbolisms, signs and codes that surround us in our communities, and affect our lives in the way we communicate, and she was feeling all the aggression, episodically, of these people who had 'pre-judged' her and were 'following' some bullshit flibbertigibbet as if it were the truth.

It was not surprising, given that even the paranormal lied, that she had less and less to believe in, apart from a women's solicitor somewhere who could deal with the rape charge and fight, the psychological torture, and the guilt tripping. It all made her feel like many people had been put against her and she was living the nightmare everywhere she went. That was paranoia again, but it doesn't mean they're not out to get you, she thought.

~

When the voices were shouting things she couldn't understand, on and on saying, "...that's why you're going to be murdered," and "your murders in the system." She thought back to the rape. She wasn't getting any justice from anywhere for the three years of abuse and psychic attacks from 'the crew' and the people they brought in to hurl abuse at her. What was real was they had put her in hospital through the trauma after the rape and continued to threaten her, saying they had slandered her character and that they had spread these rumours and people were judging her by how they had portrayed her. She was having trouble with this image and was feeling paranoid about other people. Were they all conspiring? And if not, why couldn't she just see the light and rise above the bullshit of it? At base core they were jealous-minded people with xenophobic sentiments in their views. She kept mulling over this Bob Marley tattoo that the rapist had on his chest.

The biggest problem was that she was receiving these telepathic messages every day and they were threatening and the police referred her to the doctors. She needed them to make an arrest, but she could see what they were doing to her; how they had slandered her name around the pubs as part of the show; how they wanted her to "go out and parade" so, the voices said, the people could see who was going to be murdered. She didn't feel very comfortable about that, now that they said they had told the pubs she was an enemy of the state. What a load of rubbish the people believed in! "The power of lies", she thought. How the hell was she going to get her good name cleared? This was a load of rubbish they had put her through, and she knew they were enemies and they wanted the police or the State to lock her up, as they said, for "political ends". They kept saying they were, "gonna bump her family off and then go to France to bump some more 'gypsies' off". She couldn't really believe that this was happening and chose to try to soldier on with some pride in her background, because she was proud of the fairground culture and she was proud about the things she had done in her life.

She now realised that things had gone on that long; the rape not being dealt with; the police not being very helpful; the rapist and other people shouting to her that she felt helpless until she found a focus; and the Voice Hearers conference.

~

They labelled her and brandished her with lies; put a scandal about her all over the town. They kept making more things up as time went by, threatening her with violence and death, keeping her captive and bringing in the public to abuse her. This was extreme torture and violence of a psychological nature and it was all she could do just to go to the shop some days. She was degenerating and they continued to hack away at her past in verbal abuse. She had cruel enemies and this is one woman's story of her suffering through punishment and torture, finding her own truth through the journey of mental confusion and states of paranoia induced by hours of psychological abuse.

What was so difficult for her when it came to getting help from the police was that they were attacking her through the paranormal. The simple fact was that the gang had raped her in a violent and racist attack while she had been unconscious from a spiked drink they had passed to her at the party with ulterior motives. She had been innocently oblivious. She had run to a friend's for help but, they said for her to just get away from the place as this gang was evil. So the act had been violent and had instilled in her repercussions of worthlessness and powerlessness. The words continue hour by hour putting her down with abuse and guilt trips, like they had got into her head and were attacking all of her thoughts to rationalise and try to see clearly through the pain of it all. She knew they were against her on everything and had watched and waited, taunting her that she would be dead; threatening her with violence hour by hour, month after month.

Her only 'crime' was abortion, and the rest of the public scandal that ensued was based on fabrications and lies. They used the fact that she had been brought up on the fairground to hurl racist abuse and slander her character... though she had lived in flats and houses since she was 11; had got some 'A levels' after school; and worked mainly in community arts in London and in Kent; where she had gone to University; and where she had met this gang. No matter what she tried to do in her daily life, they were still there in her head – torturing her with lies and violent abuse. It was a sad situation. She had had to spend many hours reflecting on what they were saying about her, knowing that most of it was a load of rubbish and some of it was heavy guilt trips about having had abortions, when she knew that the past only leads us if we force it to... Otherwise it contains us in it's asylum with no gates. She had remembered it as a slogan from a book. Another slogan from a feminist book: "We make history or history makes us", she had even had a T-shirt printed, changing the words slightly to: "We make Her story or history makes us". Meaning that a woman's perspective is important in this society – being as it's male dominated in most respects. She thought of the song, "What's up?", with the lyrics about fighting the institutions in this "brotherhood of man". A strong song.

They kept saying that 'her death' (their concept) was 'political', but they never explained. She knew that they were just making things up as they went along to discourage her. She thought about her 3 years in London where she lived in an all woman house where they worked together on maintenance and repairs manually. She had learned carpentry, how to put windows in, plastering, painting and decorating, putting locks into doors and general household upkeep. She thought that that was what they meant by 'political', as she had been a feminist while she was there, having a boyfriend, Jon, who was sympathetic to the cause; and about abortion rights; and had supported her morally in all her endeavours. He had a book, record and t-shirt stall, which they took to festivals and gigs around Britain. He also worked with Hackney Community Transport, a dial-a-ride for the disabled, which she had had some training with to drive and get the wheelchairs in and out of the van securely for her job at Equal Play Adventure Playground for children with Mixed Abilities. They had named it that because they believed it to be more positive about special needs in a multi-cultural environment than the word disabled. She reflected that it was a political thing because years later, when she applied for a job with special needs at Strode Park Foundation in Herne Bay, they didn't recognise any of that campaign for positive representation and it wasn't that multi-cultural.

She had contemplated the issue of a woman's rights over her own body and had remembered feeling angry on reading something in the New Scientist about these male Doctors having all these opinions on Women's Reproductive Rights like they owned them; and as if they had some deep understanding of how it is to be a woman surviving in this world. But she didn't want to lose faith. Sometimes it can be all you have left. She had always felt in control of her life before the rape had caused her a sort of 'Post traumatic Stress Disorder' and the effects of the intense psychic attacks. Her stay in hospital and the continued threats on her life had been taking its toll on her physical health and making her depressed. Hanging on to the Rape Crisis Centre and the Police reassurance for some psychological protection – trying to ward off the violent nature of their power trip over her – she had always felt kind of 'autonomous' in her private life; being creative and keeping abreast of current affairs, listening to woman's hour on Radio 4, aspiring to write radio plays as employment... all those things that she didn't achieve seemed to be out of reach in the state of mind that she'd been put under since the rape.

She remembered how much life and energy she had had... cycling everywhere in London and eating a whole food vegan diet. She had taken an 11 week course in Tai Chi at the East West Centre in Old Ford Road and found that balancing her body through work in the day was making everything else more clear. She took her bike to bits and cleaned the bearings every month, cooked creatively for her housemates once a week – as was the rota, and felt like her life was full and her mind was learning new things all the time. About different cultures, current affairs, local and global issues and working with special needs and a whole food shop on Saturdays called 'Peacemeal'. She had read through some of the pamphlet and books on Buddhist meditation and Chinese ways of healing, whole food cooking, and about grains and beans, soya and herbal remedies. She felt like she could do with some rescue remedy right now.

It was difficult to think outside of the cocoon they had built around her life; presenting her with visions of her death, and using psychological terrorism to inflict mental torture. She knew she didn't deserve all this, and that it was a scam and a power trip. She really didn't know where to start with the issues she was facing all at once. She felt like forming her own political party. She had remembered reading: 'A woman in your own right', that had exercises and plans to observe yourself and gain confidence from your self knowledge. She had had some grounding experiences in life which had taught her to try to remain calm and rational when things got chaotic – always trying for 'assertive' instead of 'passive' or 'aggressive'. But, found herself feeling angry at the taunting and threats and, at other times passive, to the mental torture which made her feel ill and drained, but mostly in a state of confusion as to how to fight them off. It seemed like they had been jealous of her; didn't like the fact that she had come from a fairground family and wanted to make her a 'victim' in society; so had built up a scandal to discredit her, brandishing her a "slut". She was traumatised by the whole affair and what it was doing to her... her life and the people who were close to her... her family, friends, and the travelling community.

"Pikey minger, we're coming to get you!" said the rapist. It was all she could do to see through all these labels and work out why the hell people can get away with this kind of racial abuse. It all seemed psychotic, violent, and very demoralising. She thought back to school when, for a short time, she had been labelled 'Kizzy', after a character of a gypsy girl on children's TV back in the 70's. It had singled her out along with the few coloured pupils, but she had never felt that it was meant in a derogatory nature and had thought positively about her time at Willowgarth High School in Grimethorpe; being good in Office Practice, Typing, Art, English and English Literature, P.E. and Drama and having a good group of friends. Lately, she felt like Sylvia Plath, writing heavy morbid poetry under the spell of being 'victimised'. She thought that it was a clash of realities, the guilt tripping and murder threats were given in a mental state of 'superiority'; a power trip, chemically induced; aggressive and egocentric. The rapist had used charismatic tactics and she was doubting the role religion played in his mind, like he thought he was Jesus or something on his 'moral crusade'. She wondered how many other women had been prey to his ritual and tried to keep faith that her soul would be safe as it was before.

As a child she had a special relationship with Jesus, having a picture on the wall where she stayed with her Grandma and Aunty in a house in Goldthorpe when she was a child. There was also a Leeds United flag and a clock inside a guitar made from a brass metal in their room. There was a big garden with lots of rockeries and different flower beds that her and her sister used to help to plant. Her Granddad lived at the bottom of a garden in a showmen's living wagon that was shaped like those American train carriages from the westerns, with raised skylights, and made of wood mostly, but painted in showmen style. He would take them on walks in the countryside nearby, through the gate he used to call 'yonder', and she always thought of the Dearne lake as 'yonder'. He had built up a permanent juvenile ride – the kind made up from cars, buses, bikes and horses – that was generated by a winding wheel in the centre. And he used to stand there, wheeling them round. There was always plenty for them to do there – having a large room with a billiard table that doubled up as a dinner table for parties and family occasions, that they used to play in. With toys that had been prizes on the bingo where her aunty worked – like the walking talking doll, desks and blackboards, toy keyboards and a guitar. She had good memories about that house.

The rapist was saying that she had served her purpose to him as a "slut" and that he was talented and serving Britain. He said that he had loads of people on his side against her and her family. He kept saying it was a horror show and that she had never grown up. She felt very scared about her safety. The things they kept saying to her were making her paranoid to go outside. They had made it feel unsafe for her, though she knew that this was his power trip over people's faith in aspects of Catholic opinion, and that there are divisions, and that it simply could not be true that all the people think the same... and she knew that she needed help to defend herself against those who were under his influence. She could sense he was making himself a reputation in using her as a power tool, so that she was being seen as a 'slut'. She pondered on language again, that the word slut had a positive meaning in the male dominated world, that she hadn't seen herself in that way and now she had been brandished such that her feminist views seemed to mean nothing and this power trip over her was making her feel self-conscious. She knew it was because she was older than him and his gang, so it was ageist as well as racist. Anyhow, all these labels were degrading and brought about to ruin her life.

"This lynching's hard mate." says the rapist. He had been talking to her for hours about what he had done to ruin her reputation and how he'd slandered her character and had turned people against her. She was feeling hurt and he kept her in pain. Every time she tried to do something he attacked her again, saying that it wasn't enough pain. She was beside herself with his taunting, as he was preying again and again on her conscience and guilt tripping her about her past. She really didn't care about his views on abortion. She had the rights and a partner in the decision and it was all legal. It was something he was using against her to make her look bad and to torture her, saying they had taken her soul in the rape – though she didn't believe it as they had lied so much about other things. He had certainly given the people something to talk about. She had wanted to give the people some music that related to her defence, in her own attempt to show that she could defend herself. The voices were saying that he was hungry and that he was powerful. He was shouting again at the fact that "it was all over the place" – this stuff about her. She was very scared and it sounded like he was on drugs, as he was frenzied and a bit psychotic. It kept going on, over and over again, calling her a Jew – which was untrue; it was a part of his power ideology, part of his evil nature. She had heard him being called a 'wild card' in Kent before she had known of him. She saw her mistake too late and realised that all along he had had ulterior motives.

"We're gonna make a film about this stuff and live off it for the rest of our lives." says the rapist. She guessed he was on drugs again, as he sounded excited. "You're getting linked off" he continued. This was heavy stuff. "There's nothing you can do about it. We've got all this power against you." She could see that they had forced her into hospital in the first place and that it had rendered her vulnerable and left her with the stigma of 'mental health patient'. She could sense that things were getting worse for her. The Police weren't taking her seriously. She had been raped, tortured and abused and there was no help. They had built up a prison around her and were using these fabrications and lies about her for their own evil ends.

She remembered reading, 'Woman on the edge of time', which was about a woman in a mental institution who travels into the future on Lithium and joins a society where everything is equal and everybody all wears the same clothes. It was about the structure of a utopian society. Somehow, it comforted her that there can still be an imagination to write the stuff after a bout in hospital; a kind of mental link to freedom of thought... though her heart felt heavy with all the verbal attacks and she found it difficult to be as creative in thought as she used to be: writing sketches and plays; working out storyboards for a film she wanted to make about travellers... but all that was before the rape. The stuff she felt now was just too heavy to make light about and her confidence had been discouraged. She kept remembering footage about the war and the persecution of gypsies.

"It's your death and I'm here to give you pain." says a voice. It is the rapist. She doesn't know how to block out the voices, but she knows there is no medication and the fear deepens as the threats get worse. "We're here to punish you for your sins." says the girl. Her thoughts go straight to the "guilt trip" they are putting on her and then to some lyrics of a band: "Freedom of conscience keeps you alive". And she knew her conscience had been struck and that she had to deal with the pressure of opposition. It was heavy and she had been suffering this guilt trip for months. She thought of music, her oil paintings, her babbling songs, her 3 guitar tunes, her work with children, her work in the community arts centres, schools, and her involvement with drama and theatre, music and dance. She attended shows and plays, concerts and parties, with her family, and felt that the scandal that the voices had talked about was out there in the community and being used for entertainment value. She felt it difficult to see the joke in this present state of mind. She wanted to write a play about it, but it seemed like the themes of violence had already been done at the local playhouse – or at least that's the way it felt – the violence the voices had threatened.

All her experiences were getting more like a David Lynch movie than real life drama. It made her think of a feminist writer called Valerie Solanas, who shot and wounded Andy Warhol, putting a stray bullet into a silkscreen of Marylin Monroe, and she wondered what could have made her so violent that she would turn on a friend... though she was known to write radically about feminism. It must have been a great artistic difference! She also remembered reading the words of Ruth Ellis: "I had a peculiar idea I wanted to kill him." on giving a statement after murdering David Bently, and she thought that it really must take a lot of courage to want to get revenge and suffer the consequences. It was a peculiar idea.

The voices were telling her to "link off", again. They often reminded her that suicide was an option out of their captivity. She always thought of it as a test of strength. She knew it was a fight and that they were using any vulnerability she had to dissuade her from building up her own reality – saying that this 'lynching' was her fate. But, she knew this was all a fabrication of truth and defamation of character. She just hadn't had the power enough to stop it from interfering with her life and future plans – since they had brandished her "the slut", "pikey", spread slander, and were generally intent on humiliating her under public scrutiny. In her mind she knew she wasn't intended to be a 'victim' and she fought the paranoia off with thoughts of her achievements in life; her ambitions, determination, and her right to say.

~

The Voice Hearers groups she had been attending had all said it was the trauma of the rape that brought it all on; all the different voices. But, she couldn't believe that totally. She still felt that they were psychic attacks. With threats on her life daily, it made her all too anxious about the State, as well as her fears for her life. The voices were always telling her they were in control and asking her to do things – then saying there was a month left to live. She was told this all the time. "We're gonna do a murder and it's you." they told her nearly everyday.

James thinks all the abuse and name calling is character assassination – saying there's a month left of the abuse – so it was like a sentence.

Jakie Dillon from the Voice Hearers said you had to take note and listen to the voices and more or less that it was no use in 'dampening them down' with medication. Now she was trying to write something down and they were saying: "What do you think happens once you've droned on about it?" as if what she thought about herself made no difference to the voices. They were still saying she had a month left and that they had "licked" her soul. This made her want to write down something about her childhood; how good it was.

It was a fact that the Voices Hearing Network said that the voices can come from many sources – birds or other animals; the rustling of leaves; traffic noise; banging hot water pipes; crowd noise; machinery noise; and even air conditioning. The most common explanations from voice hearers are that they are voices of spirits; of dead people; daemons; angels; telepathy; God-like beings; unidentified invisible beings from other dimensions; or planets... and the professional explanations of voices are: Voices come from the brain; or that voices are from the tricks of the mind when it is bored or under influence of suggestion.

Her own explanation was that it was telepathy. The voices were persecutory in the eyes of the professionals. But to her, they were giving the illusion that she was under Political pressure in that, they were saying words of abuse and threatening her life every day. She was aware that she lived in another world from her voices and that these threats of crowds being against her were not really real and in her confusion, she tried to write to express these feelings of persecution. So that maybe, there would be some comfort in other people knowing that these were small-minded fascistic type people and violent in their threats. She had not enough evidence to file a rape charge against the rapist. All she had was her own words in the confusion of theirs.

My experiences proved to me that the power of the system, being it old, is intrinsically (fascist).

One of the CPNs had come through in the voices. She was hell bent on this séance being 'SPONDULIX' as heard in the ad 'go compare'. She was really racist and fascistic in what she was saying to Imogen. They called her Lynn Robson and Imogen didn't know why she was employed in such a job with all she was saying... Then, Imogen remembered the hospital and how a lot of the workers were a little power crazed having it over others – something that Imogen hated because of her 3 years in London. It taught her a lot about people, having a job in special needs care working. The policies were different, you didn't abuse your position in the way that Lynn was doing. She'd put up with this verbal abuse now for six years. She wondered when the hell it was going to stop.

It was like psychological terrorism. She was trying to distance herself from the trauma; a war on her. Saying they had ten (meaning her family) saying they were speaking to ten when they were speaking to her. It was mental abuse in its worse sense. If she could have only made it with the Police. But, as soon as the voices were mentioned, that was it and she was referred back to the hospital. He [zac] had gotten away with the rape and he was threatening murder.

―――――――――――――――――――

www.ingramcontent.com/pod-product-compliance
Lightning Source LLC
Chambersburg PA
CBHW031439040426
42444CB00006B/881